KESTREL

ANCIENT ECHOES / SILENT MESSENGERS

an exhibition of sculpture
and drawings by

STEVE KESTREL

Introduction by J. Richard Gruber, Director

A Conversation with Steve Kestrel
by Novelene Ross, Chief Curator

WICHITA ART MUSEUM

This catalogue is supported by the City of Wichita.

ANCIENT ECHOES/ SILENT MESSENGERS

Wichita Art Museum
July 21 - September 8, 1991

Coordinated by J. Richard Gruber and
Novelene Ross

Photography by Joe Coca and Fabrice

Designed by Ken Blankinship, Steve Cooper
Higher Graphics, Inc.

Printing by Donlevy Lithograph

ISBN 0-939324-43-1

August, 1991
For Don and Donna,
With many thanks
for your interest and
support—
Steve

Portrait of the artist
Steve Kestrel, 1991.

Cover: BLACK ORBIS, slate, 1985.

cover printed on recycled paper.

INTRODUCTION

"My aim is to produce a sculpture feeling as direct and swift as a drawing, a sculpture with such ease, freedom and simplicity that it hardly feels carved, but rather to have always been that way. That accounts for the preference for field stone. Its very rudeness seems to me more in harmony with simple direct statement."

-John Flannagan, 1929

"Art is the expression of mankind, a universal and cosmic expression of the soul, an expression of the realness of the universe and life. Art is the soul of man, ever striving, ever straining toward some fulfillment, some consciousness of itself and life...."

-William Zorach, 1921

In the years after World War I, John Flannagan, William Zorach, José de Creeft and a number of other modernists sought to create a new American sculpture. Individually, they worked to transcend prevailing academic principles, evident in heroic bronze monuments and architectural sculpture, which embodied the nationalistic aspirations and high moral principles of the earlier American Renaissance period. Through the revival of direct carving, which allowed the artist to gain inspiration from the nature of the material, these American modernists advocated the creation of sculpture based upon simplification and the abstraction of natural forms.

The sculpture of Steve Kestrel suggests a bridge, a spiritual, if not literal, connection linking the concerns of these early modernists to the sculpture of the late twentieth century. In the 1990s, appreciation of the pioneering contributions of these sculptors remains limited. During my first conversation with the artist, held in the Colorado mountains in the summer of 1990, I commented upon the timeless, almost classical, nature of his work and asked if there were artists he acknowledged as influences. In response, he expressed a strong affinity for the sculpture of José de Creeft, William Zorach and John Flannagan.

Since that first conversation, it has become evident that the sculpture of Boris Gilbertson (1907-1982), played a critical role in Kestrel's aesthetic development (see the accompanying conversation with Novelene Ross). Gilbertson, who was actively involved in the development of the 1930s tradition of direct carving, moved to Santa Fe, New Mexico, in 1960 and lived there until his death. Kestrel met and worked with Gilbertson in Santa Fe during the last years of the artist's life, and, after his death, turned to direct carving using many of the tools originally owned and used by Gilbertson.

Madonna of the Trilobites (1983) and ***Golden Bough*** (1983), two of the earliest works included in this exhibition, were completed in the year following Gilbertson's death. They show a remarkable carving facility and an equally fine sense of design. Works as different as ***Black Orbis***, carved in slate in 1985, and ***Lynx Stone***, carved from river stone in 1988, demonstrate his confidence and advancing mastery of this medium. ***Lynx Stone***, in particular, reflects and updates the tradition of carving animals from field stones advanced by John Flannagan during the 1920s and 1930s.

Kestrel, unlike some of the direct carvers of the 1930s, does not limit himself to work in stone. Challenged by the creative possibilities available in foundry technologies, he plans and executes major pieces in bronze. Powerful and technically refined bronze works, including ***Aegis of the Great Circle*** (1986) and ***Spectre of Ancient Pathways*** (1988 & 1989), reflect his vision as a carver and his sensitivity to materials while taking full advantage of the inherent qualities of modern bronze casting.

Like the legendary association of Georgia O'Keeffe to her beloved New Mexico, Kestrel is closely rooted, in his art and in his life, to place. D.H. Lawrence, whose connections to Taos and northern New Mexico were well established, referred to the "spirit of place" in America's creative life. Kestrel's place is northern Colorado. He lives and works in Ft. Collins, on the edge of the Great Plains, at the base of the Rocky Mountains. Nearby is the Big Thompson Canyon which leads countless visitors each year into the mountains above Estes Park and into Rocky Mountain National Park. In this canyon he finds many of the river stones which fill his studio. In Loveland, at the mouth of the canyon, and a short drive from Ft. Collins, is his foundry. It is difficult to imagine Kestrel apart from this environment.

The landscape of the American West has inspired artists and continually influenced the evolution of American art and creative thinking. However, that landscape has undergone profound and often disturbing changes, especially in recent decades. Rooted in this western environment, and deeply concerned about the preservation of delicate ecological balances, Kestrel researches, plans and creates art forms which subtly but inescapably connect modern audiences to the natural history of the region and to the larger cycles of the American environment. As evident in the artist's catalogue comments on such pieces as ***Circle of Cranes, Owl in Winding Cloth*** and ***Passages/Desert Iguanas***, his elegant forms reflect layers of meaning, especially relating to his exploration of the relationship between man and nature.

William Zorach, one of the many artists and writers who explored the relationship between the spiritual and art in the aftermath of World War I, declared that art was "the soul of man, ever striving, ever straining toward some fulfillment, some consciousness of itself and life." Now, approaching the end of the twentieth century, there is evidence of an increasing interest in the relationship between art and the spiritual. ***Ancient Echoes/Silent Messengers*** incorporates a focused range of sculpture produced by Steve Kestrel in the period from 1983 to 1991. In these years, he has developed a vocabulary of natural forms, often very simple forms, which reverberate with references to the order of nature and art. Inherent in these references are larger implications regarding man's relationship to the world of the spirit. As is his manner, Kestrel points quietly, yet forcefully, to these larger concerns in diverse ways. Seemingly timeless, but very much a part of our current environment, Kestrel's ***Silent Messengers*** contribute, in a variety of important ways, to the evolution of contemporary sculptural traditions and to our ongoing dialogue with the natural world during the 1990s.

J.Richard Gruber
Director

A CONVERSATION WITH STEVE KESTREL
BY NOVELENE ROSS

MAY 24, 1991

Steve Kestrel is one of those artists whose personality corresponds to certain qualities in his art. We met for the beginning of this interview in Kestrel's Ft. Collins studio which is located in a warehouse behind a furniture store. His work space immediately impresses one with its neatness. Upon closer scrutiny it reveals itself to be densely occupied by the artifacts of the artist's labor and thought, his curiosity and wanderings. A cache of river stones lies piled along one wall, 2 x 8 board shelves holding bones, fossils, rocks, old taxidermists' specimens and books hang above the worn but sturdy furnishings of desk and easy chair, clean areas of well swept concrete floor surround islands of machinery and tables laden with models and tools.

Like his working quarters, Kestrel is rugged and reserved. He doesn't talk comfortably about himself or his sculpture, not because he doesn't have something to say -- as his notes for the checklist demonstrate -- but because he resists easy or superficial revelations. The artisans at the foundry where Kestrel takes his work to be cast described him as a perfectionist. In this interview he declares his pleasure in the prosaic labor of carving, his pride in his craftsmanship and his independent mastery of a multitude of techniques. Kestrel's perfectionism goes deeper than his skills and working habits, however. It also conditions his attitudes toward his subject matter.

Kestrel grew up in New Mexico participating in outdoor activities such as hiking and climbing. Through both study and experience he acquired a serious knowledge of wildlife. When Kestrel develops his sculptural conceptions of animals he demands of himself a certain accuracy in the posture and anatomy of a creature. That knowledge, however, is only a point of departure in the artist's search for a more fundamental understanding of the universal perfection of nature. Kestrel's real subjects are the patterns, rhythms, and formal harmonies of nature -- a kind of perfection which he intends to stand as a rebuke to the profligacy of man.

NR: *Why are you attracted to stone?*

SK: Having grown up in Alamagordo, New Mexico, which is at the foot of the Sacramento Mountains, I used to do a lot of hiking and climbing and later on I ended up doing quite a bit of technical rock climbing around Ft. Collins and Boulder, Colorado.

I just have an attraction to stone masses and rocky canyons -- regions like the Escalante Wilderness in southern Utah. When I was a kid I used to hike into some of the rock canyons in the Sacramento Mountains. Even then I was in awe of all that stone and its fossils.

When I was at Colorado State University I thought I was going to be a veterinarian; I was in pre-vet medicine. But I had always been interested in art and also anthropology and archaeology. So ancient stone carvings really interested me as a kid. When I was about 20 I just switched my interest from veterinary medicine to art and sculpture. For me it was a natural progression.

NR: *Well I would imagine that if you were interested in archaeology and in the past you would feel an aesthetic attraction to stone and stone carving. Did you deliberately study any past cultures?*

SK: A little bit. Pre-Columbian cultures, the Olmec, Egyptians, Assyrians, and some of the older East Indian stone carvings and sandstone carvings.

NR: *I was trying to explore some of the background for your interest in carving and also in ancient imagery, although what I've read about your work suggests that you're not specifically influenced by any particular cultural style of the past. Is that correct?*

SK: Yes.

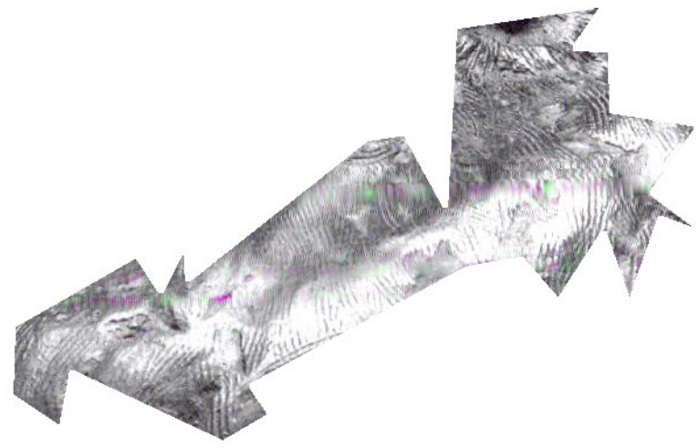

Trickster, detail, cast bronze, 1985.

NR: *Are there any modern artists who have influenced your work?*

SK: One person that really influenced my direction was Boris Gilbertson, whom I met while living in Santa Fe. Boris was from the Chicago area originally. While living in the upper Wisconsin woods before World War II, he did a number of stone-carving projects, including the large stone panels for the U.S. Department of the Interior in Washington, D.C. Boris was the only person I had known who had carved slate. He is definitely a person I consider a mentor in terms of spirit, direction, technique, tools, and practical things. I worked in Boris's studio for about two years after he died, and most of my tools were his. There are other sculptors whose work I admired. Boris was a direct carver, but that school started early in the century in this country by José de Creeft, then after that John Flannagan and William Zorach to some degree.

NR: *Were you a kind of an apprentice to Boris? Did he teach you how to carve?*

SK: By the time I met Boris in Santa Fe, New Mexico in 1980, through George Carlson, Boris was in failing health, but still producing some work. He was a great source of inspiration and information; we spent many hours talking, looking at the pieces he kept in his own collection, discussing technique and philosophy. When I met Boris, the vast majority of his life work was complete. What I was able to draw upon was the spirit of that work and the man who created it.

NR: *When did you start carving?*

SK: In 1982 I returned to Santa Fe after spending a year in Idaho building George Carlson's house. Boris's wife Charlotte White needed help cleaning out Boris's studio. I traded quite a bit of work around her place (it's an historic landmark, the first governor of New Mexico's house) and I traded for most of Boris's tools. He had an old gasoline compressor, air hammers, and many chisels. So I just cranked up the compressor and plugged in the air hammer to see how it worked. That's basically it. I have always enjoyed working with tools; I have an aptitude I think for mechanics.

NR: *Have you done construction work or design?*

SK: I had been designing and building handmade furniture for 7 or 8 years before I built two houses. The first house was in Santa Fe and was an adobe with 12 different kinds of wood that went into doors, tambours, special cabinets, and things like that. The house in Idaho that we built for George Carlson was a two story house that was very unique. It was built somewhat like Carl Larsson's, the Swedish painter's house. We brought a semi-load full of logs and had them sawn, planed, dried, and made all the floors, window trim. Every single piece of wood in the place had to have something done to it. So it was a fairly fancy house.

NR: *I'm interested in your working ideas for stone. How do you develop the piece?*

SK: It works a lot of different ways. For the stone ***Trickster*** I had a general idea what I wanted to do. I started drawing on it with chalk which is the same way I did the granite ***Lynx Stone***, and never did any preliminary drawings for either one of those. Just started drawing right on the stone with chalk. Once you decide that's the line you want you go back in with the grease pencil, it's more permanent. It is just a matter of going slow and moving the stone and keeping the silhouette of what you want on the edge. As you go deeper into it you start to lose that outline. You have to be extremely aware of where an edge goes to.

NR: *You have developed a template for certain pieces, but you don't have to have that or you don't always have that, is that correct?*

SK: Right. For some of the reliefs, in particular, it is nice to have a template. It is easy to lose an edge. For a piece like the ***Lynx Stone*** there were a few little templates used here and there on it but basically you think three-dimensionally and kind of figure out where you are going with it. The thing is, with a piece like that, by the time it's done you know it like the back of your hand.

NR: *You must have an aptitude for thinking three-dimensionally as well as for tools.*

SK: Yes, I think so. It was kind of funny, I was terrible at algebra but I did very well at geometry. It must have something to do with being able to think "form." I can close my eyes and actually visualize a piece and turn it in the air and see all the angles; that helps in terms of carving. The field stone or river stone is more organic in shape than blocks and I know that many other sculptors have said the same thing, but it does suggest shapes to you. It is much more exciting and interesting than a rectangle or a cube.

NR: *You do go out and search for some of this material, the granite particularly?*

SK: I probably have twice as much in storage or marked as what was in the studio. I have a kind of backlog of pieces I can always refer to. It's nice to have a lot of different things to pick from; then you don't have to feel it's so precious that you can't experiment.

NR: *Where have you located some of this river stone?*

SK: The bulk of the river stones come from the Cache La Poudre River and I think probably that the lowest down I found that I could use was about 5 miles from the mouth of the canyon and as far up as a little above Kelly Flats. The best pieces are in the water farthest from the van and also the largest and hardest to carry.

NR: *And then for the bison piece,* ***Spectre of Ancient Pathways****, you went to South Dakota to take photographs. Where in South Dakota?*

SK: Custer State Park, South Dakota.

NR: *In that case you were doing some field research. Do you like to work that way? Do you want to examine an animal or find a context or a particular departure point for a piece?*

SK: I think you have to know the animal well enough so that you get all the major landmarks, the features that make a bison a bison, or a lynx a lynx. And then the art part comes in interpreting that and in doing something different with it. I guess I'll put it this way. I'm never going to create a buffalo. Those animals have muscles and veins and bones.

So I can never duplicate that. The best painter or the best sculptor in the world will never be able to duplicate that either. So what I am trying to do is create something that, in a sense, is a different animal, but at the same time using reference points.

NR: *You have reference points in nature, but at the same time you are not trying simply to document nature?*

SK: There is enough of that. That's been done and been done well. And I don't knock some of the sculptors or painters who have done that in the past, especially if they were pushing their medium at the time and they were the innovators. The people who have come after them and copied them and driven it into the ground, I don't respect them. People that have taken an idea or an image and pushed it in a new direction are the ones I like to think that I identify with.

NR: *Yet you were also saying earlier that you didn't like things that were too slick or too refined.*

SK: Yes, that's fair. There is so much bad art in the magazines today that is nauseating. They are gimmicky, trendy and slick. These people get images and they just drive them into the ground and do them over, over and over again. I want to stay away, far away from those people. I think they are in it for the money, they are in it for the short run. A lot of those people, it's the cult of their personality that lets them be so successful. They are good business people first, and artists somewhere down the line, maybe tenth on the list.

NR: *You are really interested in quality, too. We saw that today from your comments at the foundry and from the comments of the foundry men about you that you are very picky; you really look, handle the work, supervising its development all the way.*

SK: It is part of the legacy you leave. The artwork is going to be here a lot longer than any of us. So I would like it to be as perfect as it can be.

NR: *I feel that idea expresses your concepts too because the forms in which your animals finally emerge are not naturalistic or accidental ones. The quick and ephemeral movement isn't quite your thing either. The forms suggest the eternal and lasting. Is that something you are consciously seeking?*

SK: I think so, I hope so -- something that has a more universal appeal says something more than the mere depiction of an animal.

NR: *You use a lot of birds in your work. Is there a particular fascination with birds and also reptiles?*

SK: They are both very good sculptural material. I tend to be drawn toward repeating

Spectre of Ancient Pathways, cast bronze, 1988.

patterns. Birds are an obvious, easy one for that -- the feather structure -- and the same with some of the reptiles. They are kind of at opposite ends of poles, one in the air and one on the ground.

NR: *Tell me about a specific piece, the one which you are working on now. The as yet unnamed hybrid wolf. Can you tell me how you got started on that piece, what gave you the idea and how you developed it?*

Ancient Echoes, *cast bronze, 1991.*

SK: I think the pose was what got me. That pose.

NR: *How did you get into the subject? What sparked the choice of that particular animal?*

SK: That was Boris and Charlotte's hybrid wolf Chica. When wolves have their ears back, their vision is focused forward but they are listening behind themselves. Cindi and I were talking about the piece the other day in relation to a title. We were both commenting on the fact that when she's (the wolf piece) looking forward like that, that can indicate the present or the future, but the ears to the back would indicate the past. So we are going to try to tie that into some kind of a title.

It is just interesting all the different things that have been going on in the last couple of years -- it is not why I did the piece -- with wolves being introduced into national parks and all that controversy that is going on in terms of Yellowstone. And there is quite a bit of controversy about hybrid wolves also. Between just an interest in wolves and interest in a particular -- and Chica was the first hybrid wolf I had ever known -- I set out to take photos of Chica, probably in 1983. I have mainly worked from black and white photos that I took then; I have been to Santa Fe a couple of times this winter and used her for a model and took more photos.

NR: *Was it your feeling for the people who owned it as well as the animal which inspired the piece?*

SK: Both, but mainly the animal. She's an extremely unique animal, a timber wolf. The thing that was strange about Chica was that she would make up to women fairly quickly. And Boris was the only male she accepted -- I was the second one and it happened very quickly. I think that's why we all got along so well. So I felt like that was a really special relationship. She is over 14 years old now and not doing very well, but she's a beautiful, beautiful animal. Very unusual. They have a real thing about eye contact. When they meet new people they don't want the people to stare at them. That's challenging to them. You just don't do that.

NR: *In that particular piece then, you portray the personality of the animal type?*

SK: Yes, somewhat. I have tried to get further away from hybrid wolf to wolf so that it doesn't confuse the whole thing. I'd rather have the piece just read as wolf rather than as dog or hybrid wolf.

NR: *When you do animal pieces do you think of a species representing an ideal or certain qualities?*

SK: To some degree. I find the ***Trickster*** (raven) is probably a good one for that. There is a double-fold meaning to their personalities -- good and evil, comical and sinister all wrapped into one. I wrote about the ***Trickster*** and quoted Paul Radin in that and he had a wonderful couple of paragraphs which says it even better -- "dual presences" embodied in the same animal.

NR: *So there are qualities in your pieces which may be literary, may belong not only to the natural character of these creatures, but also to their historic and mythological characters?*

SK: Yes, it is the same way with the bison. The North American Plains Indian cultures were for the most part built around the bison, and that piece (***Sceptre of Ancient Pathways***) also has a lot of connections to paleolithic cave paintings. And the other thing I was trying to get out of that piece was an archetypal image, an egg shape, a closed shape. There are some people who ask me why I didn't open it up between the legs; I just wanted the nice closed shape. Part of that comes from stone carving because stones are basically closed shapes. I could never do the ***Circle of Cranes*** in stone; it just wouldn't work. That's an open, fragile shape.

Circle of Cranes, cast bronze and granite, 1988.

NR: *Cranes, owls, and snakes are all animals with a pretty powerful imagistic history and usage. But I take it you are not working like an anthropologist to resurrect specific references; it's more general.*

SK: Yes, I would say it's more general. I try not to be too specific so that the piece can be enjoyed and it has many different layers of meaning. There are many sculptures that if you own one of them for 10 minutes you are probably going to know everything you can know about that particular piece. If you owned it for another fifty years you are not going to know anything more. I would hope that my pieces would intrigue people for a number of years.

NR: *The relief carvings which you do obviously have a background. How do you think in terms of relating figure to background?*

SK: The most recent one is the slate carving of the rattlesnake and the lizard. In the slate I call it ***Black Sand Monolith***. In the bronze I am calling it ***Desert Solitaire***. I have always wanted to do some predator -- prey relationship kinds of things because they just interest me. I really enjoyed working with the abstract quality of the edge of that piece where the repeating shapes taper up to

Desert Solitare, (recto & verso) cast bronze, 1990.

the top also. At the top of the piece the tail folds over all the way and there are just some nice little surprises. I had a lot of fun working on it. That's not what I would call a heavy-duty philosophical piece, and yet it's not a whimsical piece either. That piece was really enjoyable to do, technically challenging. Probably one of the most challenging pieces I have ever done.

NR: *Why was that?*

SK: Because it's slate.

NR: *Talk a little bit about the difficulties or joys of working with slate.*

SK: Well it's layered. It's like working with hard parchment all compressed into layers. You have to always be aware that slate is in layers and if you fracture something in the wrong way, it is going to split down the fracture. So when I first start working on a slate piece I always consciously remind myself about the nature of the material so I don't make a mistake, and after two or three days I don't have to think about it -- it becomes second nature.

NR: *How do you cut slate?*

SK: That particular slate is extremely hard; to rough it out I used diamond saws and 10" grinders on big right-angle grinders. This piece was all mapped out ahead of time with a template. Even when you know what material to remove, it is an extremely time-consuming thing because once you remove the material, that's it. And then once it is roughed out with those kinds of things -- on that particular piece I also did use a little bit of the air hammers and chisels, but you have to be real careful -- and then after that a lot of air rotary tools and hand files to get some of the final shapes. We are talking probably a good week to rough a piece like that out, and then 3-4 weeks with rotary grinders and things that refine a lot of the shapes, and then another 2-4 weeks to start to really get down to the nitty gritty of some of those details, and then maybe a week to really finish the piece.

NR: *How do you finish the surface?*

SK: Just use finer and finer grinders and sanders and a lot of hand sanding. Then, take the example of the scales on the snake -- I had to redraw those probably 4 or 5 times. I tried to figure out a system at first to do it using little tiny templates for different sizes of scales and it just didn't work and I finally just had to do it all freehand. You have to increase or decrease the size of the scales and have them all overlap just right. It took a good day just to draw the scales and another two days to grind them in.

NR: *What attracted you to bronze? You often translate stone or slate pieces into bronze. When did you start doing that?*

SK: Oh, after I had carved for a couple of years in Santa Fe, I decided it was time to try to cast a few pieces.

NR: *Did you want to do that to achieve an edition or is there something special about bronze that you like?*

SK: Well, it's a number of things. Part of it is, I would admit, economic because I am slow and it is difficult to turn out a lot of pieces every year. It varies from year to year. So part of the appeal was being able to...

NR: *Probably to support yourself better.*

SK: Yes, but obviously a piece like the ***Circle of Cranes*** had to be bronze because of its composition and structure, and I feel like there are others that are the same way. There are forms that you can't get by with in stone such as unsupported projections from the main mass. However, some stone pieces also work quite well in bronze.

NR: *How did you come to develop forms for bronze. Did you teach yourself that too?*

SK: Yes. You have a certain amount of exposure to art history books and other artists and literature and things like that. In terms of the process though it's just trial and error, going to the foundries and making stupid mistakes and learning from them. I've dealt with four different foundries now. So I've got a lot of mistakes under my belt.

NR: *You have bronzes cast from your stone and slate pieces but you also model in wax. You are, for example, making the original of the wolf piece in wax. What differences do you experience in the processes of carving and modeling?*

SK: Carving is the most time-consuming, the riskiest. You have to be in the right frame of mind to do that and it's too, for me anyway, it's too nerve shattering to do it all the time. You really have to be up to carve stone.

NR: *Because a mistake means the loss of the whole thing...*

SK: Yes; it's real time consuming, and you have to wear protection for your eyes and lungs, and you've got these machines banging along and air hammers going. You really have to know what you want to do and be ready and it just takes a lot of physical energy. Sometimes I need a change of pace, so I do modeling. I have nice, quiet music on and ...

NR: *It can be clean and ...*

SK: Yes ...

NR: *You can breathe.*

SK: It's a real great balance.

NR: *You are saying that the process of carving involves both physical and psychic labor.*

SK: Yes, and that's why I don't want to chase (grind) bronze any more. I'd rather save that kind of energy for the stone carvings.

NR: *What reward is there in doing that physical process of carving the stone?*

SK: Well, it would be the difference between playing football and billiards or something -- it's kind of rough and tumble. It can be real exciting at times when you've got all that equipment going. It's a lot of activity.

NR: *There's also the uniqueness of the object, and I would think that with your aesthetic preference for solidness and timelessness that you enjoy stone for these qualities.*

SK: Right.

NR: *There must be a sense of these qualities in the granite, the found river stones which you like to use?*

SK: Yes, to think that those formed millions and millions of years ago, laying hidden for eons . . . and then to be able to do something with them. Although at times you see a glimpse of nature which makes you feel like just laying down your tools and not ever trying to sculpt again. You can take it either way sometimes. There are some great things out there (in nature) that are just incredible and you can work and not feel bad about it. There are other times you want to lay the tools down and forget about it because human beings are so insignificant in comparison to the grandeur and beauty of nature.

Lynx Stone, granite river stone, 1988.

NR: *But there are times when nature's forms excite you?*

SK: Right.

NR: *They spur you on to work because they grab ideas inside that you see.*

SK: Yes, I think the ***Lynx Stone*** is probably a good example of that. I didn't have any other animal in mind for that piece or any other pose. That was natural.

NR: *The stone itself suggested that form?*

SK: Yes.

NR: *I've read that about stone carving and wondered if it really worked that way for some artists.*

SK: I've read that about other sculptors too. I think Flannagan and some of the others talked about having stones around for two to ten years and finally an idea would hit them. So it's great to have stones. Great to have them around and not feel like you've only got one or two left. You have a whole mess of them so that you can take some chances.

NR: *You like to be surrounded by your wealth, by all these stones, so that you feel rich.*

SK: It's like money in the bank.

NR: *Have you ever carved in wood?*

SK: I used to carve a fair amount of wood when I was still in furniture and some of my early pieces in school were carved in wood. But I've worked with woods for so long that I haven't been drawn to it since I've started doing this full time. In addition, I stay away from soft stones and ... alabaster ... it has all been overdone. And I don't like white marble. In this day and age it's too reminiscent of porcelain and plastic. It works fine for some things, but very few things, I find. There are people that have used it and have done a great job with it but it is not for me now. So ... I mainly carve granite and slate and then after that I would say limestone and sandstones.

NR: *Do those materials suggest a certain environment or place to you? Do they mean Colorado to you, for example?*

SK: The West.

NR: *And is that part of your attraction to those materials?*

SK: Yes.

NR: *Talk a little about just why you like this country.*

SK: I visited Wisconsin, but I've never been further East than that ... I got a little claustrophobic. Out here what you see is kind of what you get. The landscape is not completely covered up with foliage ... especially in New Mexico. There's just nothing else like it ... quite open ... a sense of freedom. I like being in areas of the earth that haven't been populated too awful long. Certain areas of North America have been sparsely populated as far back as 12,000 years. It is not like parts of the earth where there are places that have been heavily occupied for thousands and thousands of years and every square mile of the earth has been touched by the hand of man. And I guess that's what I like, is that it is so natural. It hasn't felt our presence. It's still wild.

NR: *Is that a feeling that you think you put into your work? I mean ... this sense of the newness of nature, newness of the West or the pristine quality of nature without the human imprint?*

SK: Yes ... I'm sure that's part of it but at the same time in some of the pieces there's also a warning. Those iguana pieces are sort of like that. I've used circles in a lot of the pieces to connote completeness, continuity and the cyclical nature of how things are ... and mankind has a way of really screwing things up a lot of times, interjecting things that upset the cycle. We all know that, I mean it's become very popular in the last 15, 20 years and it's time that it happened. I'm skeptical as to how that's all going to play out on a global scale.

NR: *I'm tempted to ask you if you think that the human species even fits into the cycle?*

SK: Well, not as well as we could. Not nearly as well as we could.

AWARDS AND RECOGNITION

National Sculpture Society - New York, NY - member
Society of Animal Artists - City Island, NY - member
Loveland High Plains Arts Council - Loveland, CO - board of directors

1991	NAWA (guest artist) National Cowboy Hall of Fame, Oklahoma City, OK
1991	Wichita Art Museum (one-man show, July 21 - Sept. 8), Wichita, KS
1991	Northwest Rendezvous Group (guest artist) Holter Museum of Art, Helena, MT
1990	"Birds in Art," Leigh Yawkey Woodson Art Museum, Wausau, WI
1990	Wildlife: The Artist's View, Leigh Yawkey Woodson Art Museum, Wausau, WI
1990-1985	"Sculpture in the Park," Loveland High Plains Arts Council, Loveland, CO
1989	National Sculpture Society, 56th Annual Exhibition, New York, NY
1989	North American Sculpture Exhibition, Golden, CO
1989	Vail Valley Arts Council Invitational Art Show, Vail, CO
1988	Allied Artists of America, 73rd Annual Exhibition, New York, NY
1988	National Sculpture Society, 55th Annual Exhibition, New York, NY (Tallix Foundry Award)
1988	"Birds in Art," Leigh Yawkey Woodson Art Museum, Wausau, WI - (Permanent collection and 1988-89 USA Tour)
1988	"Excellence '88," Texas Sculpture Association, Dallas, TX
1988	Poudre Valley Art League, 27th Annual Regional Exhibition, Fort Collins, CO (First-Place Award for Sculpture)
1988	Eagle Valley Arts Council Invitational Art Show, Vail, CO (Viewer's Choice Award and Jurors' Award)
1988	Springville Museum of Art, 64th National April Salon, Springville, UT
1986	Springville Museum of Art, 62nd National April Salon, Springville, UT (Director's and Juror's Awards)
1985	National Sculpture Society, 52nd Annual Exhibition, New York, NY
1985	"Birds in Art," Leigh Yawkey Woodson Art Museum, Wausau, WI
1985	Loveland Museum Show, Three Person, Loveland, CO
1984	One-Man Exhibition, Home of Dr. and Mrs. John Fleming, Denver, CO
1984	North American Sculpture Exhibition, Golden, CO (Colorado Sculpture Award)
1983	George Carlson Studio Show, Elizabeth, CO

PUBLIC AND PRIVATE COLLECTIONS

U.S. West Communications - Denver, CO
Leigh Yawkey Woodson Art Museum - Wausau, WI
Loveland High Plains Arts Council - Loveland, CO
Mr. and Mrs. George Carlson
Mr. and Mrs. J. R. Preston
Mr. George Getz
Mr. and Mrs. Gary Herberger
Mr. and Mrs. Mel Ritter
Dr. and Mrs. John Fleming
Dr. and Mrs. W. McIlvaine
Dr. N. Jill Warren and Dr. David Smith
Mr. and Mrs. George Walbye
Bill Bishop
Carol Siple

CHECKLIST

WITH ARTIST'S NOTES

1 ***AEGIS OF THE GREAT CIRCLE***

Cast bronze, 1986
29" x 36" x 8 1/4"
Ed.: 3/7
Lent by the artist

2 ***ANCIENT ECHOES***

Cast bronze, 1991
17 1/2" x 28 3/4" x 19 1/4"
Ed.: 1/15
Lent by the artist

1 "Many thoughts and images came to mind during the conceptual portion of this piece. The following is a condensed approximation of those thoughts.

"The disc symbolism is twofold in that it reaches back in time to several ancient cultures and their use of the solar disc for its affirmation of life and its connections to the cyclic patterns of the seasons and celestial movements. This complements my use of the disc and circle in other works to represent completeness and continuity for not only the human species, but for all of the biosphere.

"The owl images are somewhat similar in form and content to a previous piece I did called *Brujo*. But here, as mirror images of each other, the owls represent the human mind -- and as in one mind or the collective many, there occurs in ebb and flow what could be termed as the light side and the dark side. They are guardians of the disc, upon an apex in time, with their wings swept forward in a posture of potential transformation -- a gesture of the possibilities and secrets yet unrevealed."

3 *BLACK ORBIS*

Black slate, 1985
21" x 23" x 5 1/4"
Lent by Bishop Gallery/Bill & Gail Bishop, Scottsdale, AZ & Allenspark, CO

3 "To the Aztecs the rattlesnake was the 'Yellow Lord' of all snakes and symbolized the cycles of renewal and rebirth. To other cultures they represent evil, fear, and death. I thought it fitting to use both symbologies ... the snake surrounding a perfect circle: continuity and completeness, or chaos and the abyss."

4 *BROOKSTONE*

Granite river stone, 1991
3 3/4" x 15" x 13 1/2"
Lent by the artist

5 *CICADA SONG*

Cast bronze, 1990
7" x 13 1/2" x 3"
Ed.: 8/21
Lent by the artist

6 *CIRCLE OF CRANES*

Cast bronze, 1987
11" x 7" x 2 1/2"
Ed.: AP/21
Lent by Cindi Kunselman, Fort Collins, CO

6 "A few years ago I had the good fortune to observe and photograph Sandhill and Whooping Cranes at Bosque del Apache, New Mexico. At sunset, hundreds of darkly silhouetted cranes swept in from the northern cobalt sky, their call intensifying as they flew closer. With wings set, and then pounding as their extended legs neared the glistening mud flats of the marsh, a chorus of primeval chatter thickened the moment and seemed of another, more ancient time. My hope for these birds to endure and prosper in the future is embodied in this piece."

7 *CIRCLE OF CRANES*

Cast bronze and granite, 1988
66" x 28" x 6"
Ed.: 2/8
Lent by Dr. & Mrs. John Nagel, Fort Collins, CO

8 *DESERT SOLITAIRE*

Cast bronze, 1990
30" x 12" x 10"
Ed.: 1/11
Lent by the artist

9 *DUNE/SNAKE RACE*

Cast bronze, 1983
21 1/2" x 11" x 2"
Ed.: 3/8
Lent by the artist

9 "The snake is an interesting and versatile subject for works of sculpture. This is an attempt at reptilian humor -- allowing people to view the highly evolved rattlesnake with some amusement and more awe than fear."

10 GOLDEN BOUGH

New Mexico sandstone, 1983
8 1/2" x 12 1/2" x 10"
Lent by Cindi Kunselman, Fort Collins, CO

11 GOLDEN BOUGH

Cast bronze, 1985
8 1/2" x 12 1/2" x 10"
Ed.: 3/8
Lent by Bishop Gallery/Bill & Gail Bishop, Scottsdale, AZ & Allenspark, CO

12 LYNX STONE

Granite river stone, 1988
14 1/2" x 19" x 7 1/2"
Lent by Bishop Gallery/Bill & Gail Bishop, Scottsdale, AZ & Allenspark, CO

13 *MADONNA OF THE TRILOBITES*

New Mexico sandstone, 1983
17 1/2" x 10 1/2" x 9"
Lent by Mr. & Mrs. Gary Herberger, Paradise Valley, AZ

13 "A piece dedicated to the forgotten but beautiful trilobites: the first arthropods, who inhabited this planet's seas for 345 million years in some 4,000 different guises. A very stately flexicalymene from the Ordovician period patiently modeled for me."

14 *NIGHTHAWK*

Cast bronze, 1989
22" x 17" x 6"
Ed.: 1/21
Lent by Bishop Gallery/Bill & Gail Bishop, Scottsdale, AZ & Allenspark, CO

15 *OWL IN WINDING CLOTH*

Cast bronze, 1983
28" x 11" x 8"
Ed.: 3/8
Lent by Cindi Kunselman, Fort Collins, CO

15 "This piece expresses the tragedy and mystery of death -- easier reconciled in our minds with other animals in terms of evolutionary mandate, and less so concerning ourselves. It represents the death of a single being, but could it also be the death of accumulated human wisdom derived from philosophy, religion, and science? Can this wisdom which respects and understands the biosphere and our place in it still be overwhelmed by greed, apathy, ignorance, population pressures, global politics, or outdated belief systems?"

16 *PASSAGES/DESERT IGUANAS*

Cast bronze, 1984
4 1/2" x 27 1/2" x 3"
Ed.: 2/8
Lent by Tony and Shannon Hochstetler, Loveland, CO

16 "Reptiles are such an ancient and enduring life form that they evoke a feeling of continuity and completeness in me -- symbolized by the circle and line connecting the pair of Iguanas. The other side of the piece begins with the same symbol and regresses with the fracturing and 'de-evolution' of all species, if mankind's impact on the planet is not curtailed or reversed."

17 *RAINMAKER*
Cast bronze & stone, 1988
4" x 12"
Ed.: 18/21
Lent by the artist

18 *RAINMAKER STONE*
Granite river stone, hand-wrought bronze, gold plate, 1988
6" x 9 1/2" x 8"
Lent by Michael Wisdom, Wray, CO

19 *RAINMAKER TOO*
Cast bronze, 1990
4 1/2" x 10 1/2" x 9"
Ed.: 6/21
Lent by Walter Matia, Alexandria, VA

20 *SHIFTING ORBS*
Black slate, 1985
21" x 23" x 5 1/4"
Lent by Bishop Gallery/Bill & Gail Bishop, Scottsdale, AZ & Allenspark, CO

21 *SOURCE OF THE LIGHT*
Slate, [illegible]
3 1/2" x 11 1/2" x 6 1/2"
Lent by Bishop Gallery/Bill & Gail Bishop, Scottsdale, AZ & Allenspark, CO

17 "An outwardly humorous piece which may be viewed at different levels . . .

. . . the bottom thicker stone may be viewed as the cosmos -- circular, flecked and floating, while the thinner slate may represent terra-firma (Earth) with two (of many) ingredients inextricably bound which make the planet special -- life and water.

. . . circles can be symbols for perfection, continuity, harmony, beginnings meeting ends -- and are also reminiscent of the regenerative nature of embryonic cells -- cell walls, nuclei, etc. The design on the underside of the frog may be viewed as a symbol of eternity or -- if you're a kid -- simply tadpoles."

22 ***SPECTRE OF ANCIENT PATHWAYS***

Cast bronze, 1988
11 1/2" x 10 1/2" x 4"
Ed.: 6/21
Anonymous loan

23 ***SPECTRE OF ANCIENT PATHWAYS***

Cast bronze, 1989
36" x 34" x 12"
Ed.: 2/10
Lent by the artist

24 ***SPECTRE OF ANCIENT PATHWAYS***

Cast bronze, 1989
84" x 68" x 24"
Ed.: 2/6
Wichita Art Museum,
Burneta Adair Endowment Fund

25 ***TRICKSTER***

Cast bronze, 1985
27" x 5" x 6 1/2"
Ed.: 6/11
Lent by the artist

22 "My intent with *Spectre of Ancient Pathways* was to capture an archetypal image of 'bison:' an image with a somewhat raw, visceral energy rooted in both North American and European Paleolithic mythologies, art and artifacts."

25 "The mythology of the *Trickster* in his various animal and human forms is ancient and somewhat universal. To me the raven embodies the mythology best, because at one moment they appear withdrawn and sinister, the next moment inquisitive and comical. As Paul Radin has written in his book *The Trickster*, '... we are here in the presence of a figure and a theme or themes which have had a special and permanent appeal and an unusual attraction for mankind from the very beginnings of civilization. In what must be regarded as its earliest and most archaic form, as found among the North American Indians, Trickster is at one and the same time creator and destroyer, giver and negator, he who dupes others and who is always duped himself. He wills nothing consciously. At all times he is constrained to behave as he does from impulses over which he has no control. He knows neither good nor evil, yet he is responsible for both. He possesses no values, moral or social, is at the mercy of his passions and appetites, yet through his actions all values come into being.' "

26 *WATER'S EDGE*
Cast bronze & rosewood, 1984
14 1/2" x 11" x 1"
Ed.: 7/21
Lent by the artist

27 Study for ***BROKEN CIRCLES***
(for the bronze commissioned by Dr. & Mrs. John Fleming, Denver, CO)
Pencil on paper, 1984
17 1/4" x 34 1/4"
Lent by the artist

28 Study for **MESSENGER** (A Michael Mahaffey & Assoc. project for the Oklahoma Heart Center/Baptist Medical Plaza North, Oklahoma City)
Pencil on mylar, 1985
11" x 24"
Lent by the artist

29 Study for **MESSENGER** (A Michael Mahaffey & Assoc. project for the Oklahoma Heart Center/Baptist Medical Plaza North, Oklahoma City)
Pencil on mylar, 1985
11" x 24"
Lent by the artist

30 Study for **MESSENGER** (A Michael Mahaffey & Assoc. project for the Oklahoma Heart Center/Baptist Medical Plaza North, Oklahoma City)
Pencil on mylar, 1985
11" x 24"
Lent by the artist